The First 8 Months

Keri Perram

Presentation by *BookLeaf Publishing*

Web: www.bookleafpub.com

E-mail: info@bookleafpub.com

ISBN: 9789395784429

First edition 2022

Dedication

For my child

Preface

I would like to welcome you to what I like to call 'Milk on Tap' - the trendiest bar in town. Whether ordered from the tap, or the bottle, all the 'babes' are there, at all hours and the bar tenders use cute pet names to all who order... by the way, did I mention that you're one of the only two bar tenders who share a 24/7 workload?! The customers are usually okay and don't really get up to much, especially the first few weeks, where all they use your space for is to feed and sleep (oh, and pop in to the bathroom ofcourse). Sometimes they fall asleep at the bar though often complaining when you kick them out, or make them try a new mixer. Despite all this though, it's one of the best roles you're ever going to have.

day 1

There is a stranger in my home
Taking up space in my bedroom without thought to
ask
There is a stranger in my home
Taking up all my time, from one minute to the last.
There is a stranger in my home
Who begs for attention all the time
There is a stranger in my home
Who knows how to cross the line
There is a stranger in my home
They're getting bigger every day
There is a stranger in my home
I wouldn't have it any other way.

day three

I say your name.
It doesn't feel right on my lips.
Don't get me wrong, your name suits you to the tee
But you've been "my bub" for so long now
Saying the title we decided on only once you became
earthside is like a foreign body.
I pronounce it slowly, getting used to the feel of it in
my mouth.
I sign cards, looking at how our family's names are
coming together in written form.
I tell people who you are. That you are my child.
That I am your mother.
That I am anyone's mother is flabbergasting enough,
but I am Your mother. My husband and I named you.
Your father and mother named you.
You have a name.
You are a child
I am a mother
I have a child. A baby.
I say your name again.

Day 7

It's dark
My ears ringing into the silence of the night.
Not silence.
Hubby snores in the next room as I sway on the new glider chair, glad I bought it.
Not silence.
Sucking and swallowing emanating from this leech attached to my breast.
Did I just call my newborn a leech?
Is that bad? Leeches are used to heal, they take their feed and then go on their way.
The leech sucks my milk, specially created and formulated to their specific needs.
The leech sucks my time. How is it already tomorrow? Where did yesterday go?
The leech sucks my energy. Draining me dry until all I can do is sleep. Except I can't because
The leech sucks my sleep, needing attention and care and love for so much of each day.
And night.
The dark reminds me of the leech.
The leech is my future.
The leech is my everything.
I love my leech.

Week 3

5

A cow
Tits out to the world
But don't show too much skin less you disturb an
onlooker at the farm
Milked by mouth and machine
The liquid gold not gold anymore but just as
valuable, if not moreso.
We are made for this.
The ultimate sacrifice for our child.
Not sacrifice.
Gift.
And though the comparison to the four legged beauty
is uncanny
I will not be shamed.

Week six

The book says this
The Web says that
The nurses are saying something else
But a mum in my group heard from their friend the opposite
"Each child is different"
But you have to fit in these parameters
"Each child is different"
But if they can't do this yet then they're 'slow' to learn.
"Each child is different"
But you shouldn't cosleep
"Each child is different"
But you shouldn't leave them in their own cot
"Each child is different"
But...
"Each child is different"
But...
"Each child is different"
....
Perhaps each parent is different too.

12 weeks in

7

There comes a time when things just work
You stop questioning what else there is to lurk
Around the corners from day to day
And you learn that everyone will want to have their say.
But as a new mum, you know your child best.
As a new mum, you've built your own nest.
As a new mum you've learnt your new routine.
And as a new mum you've learnt when you can lean
On others and when to hold your ground.
When to venture out and when you're homeward bound.

A Moment in Time

Did you just laugh?
Like actually though?
...
There it was again!
Such beauty and joy
Such angelic sounds beaming through the gates of
hell as I open your dirty diaper and you continue to
defecate (across the room now).
But you laughed.
And nothing you do can ruin this.

Just a thought

Innocence
So sweet as the mango all over your lips on a warm
summers day
Serenity
So pure as the happiness in your eyes, untarnished by
the world's harsh ways

4 months

Breath in
Breath out
Breath in
Breath out
Breath in In In
Deep breath out
And your whole body weight releases into my arms
as your head snuggles closer into my pit, shielding
from the light of the day during your afternoon nap in
mummas arms.
Oh, how I love these naps.

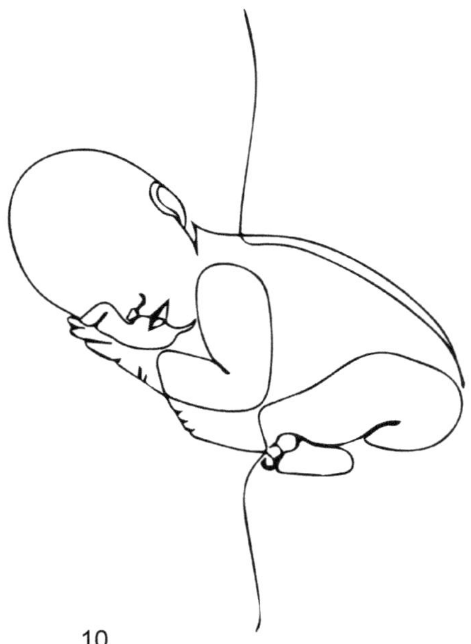

5 Months

Head slumped down,
Back hunched over,
Bags under your eyes,
Stains on your clothes
Yet as I hear you two talking:
"it's okay baby. Time for bed"
"Da da bahb maaaa"
"That's right Dada is putting you to sleep so mama
can have a rest"
You've never looked better as my eyelids eventually
give in to the weights pushing them closed.

Stream of Consciousness Lullaby

It's time to sleep my little love
As I hold you on my shoulder above
And rock and swing and sway and pat
And hope there's something...Anything that
Will help put you to sleep this day
And hold your big wet tears at bay.
Shhhh
Shhh
Shh
Sh And here we go again.

The calm sucking of fingers is not enough
For the bubble of gas. Stuck. Tough.
So we walk and we pace and we sing out of tune
Hoping all hope that you'll go to sleep soon.
But sleep is held off again on this night
For after a big burp, well you're hungry... that's right.

Almost 6 months

Like a gecko
Fingers splayed
Arms reach full extension
Slapping to the ground
Right arm
Left arm
Right leg
Left leg
Slapping the carpeted floor with your hands
Sliding your knees forward, sometimes separately
Sometimes together
Your toothless glee, not dissimilar to that of the
gecko, evident as you realise what you've achieved.

Still almost six months

14

Roll, pivot, push up your head.
Slide around the flooring, push up on the bed.
One leg, then two.
Then stuck for a few...
Two legs at once, then an arm
Your face hits the floor. But without alarm
Your back at it again.
Working to crawl from end to end

Finally, six months

We show off all your talents through videos and pictures
Redoing the house with all sorts of fixtures
For now that you've grown, your moving so much!
(Rolling and crawling and climbing and such)
You grab things with your hands
You squeal, "isn't this grand!"
Reading through your books
And practising all your looks
And every time we make a video call
It's like you want to show them off for all.

still 6 months

Why wont you sleep?
Are you too hot? Or too cold?
Why won't you sleep?
Do you want another cuddly to hold?
Why won't you sleep?
Should I put the sound to mute?
Why won't you sleep?
Do you need a thicker sleep suit?
Why won't you sleep?
Just please, rest your head.
Please go to sleep.
It's time for bed

Nearly seven months

Off to the park today
Off to the park to play
Well, 'play' might be a bit of a stretch
But we're outside, and that's the best!
Sitting on the rug, chatting away with friends
Then you look up to me: "I don't want this to end".
Oh! The joys, to move and be free.
Oh the joys to just get to be 'me'.

A Realisation

18

Motherhood is a very special kinship
Unlike anything else in the world.
We are all born with a mother, it's biologically impossibly
to say otherwise.
So to raise a child of your own brings with it a likeness to
the others in the same situation as yourself.
To raise a child takes a level of strength and patience and
wanting and teaching that, perhaps, we never thought we
would be able to endure.
To raise a child, to be a mother, is a lifestyle, not a title.
And only those who know, will know.

Seven Months

My child
My sweet child
My sweet, sweet child
How the time has past
How, with time, you've grown
No longer a newborn
Barely even a baby the way you make your needs
known
Even without the ability to speak yet
Still so determined in mind, body and spirit
Your laughter
Your tears
Your smile
All telling us what you need.
So able to communicate.
So able to love and be loved
So able to fill my heart with a strength, determination
and fight I never knew I had.
For you
My child

A Day In Between

Inside, outside, all the way around, we run and walk
and enjoy the sun
Soon to be eating, then playing some more
As the day wears on we yawn, then snore
And after our nap we do it again
Kind of hoping it will never end

Nearly 8 months

21

I hand you the cutlet
You take it, unsure
A little nibble, but not much yet
Then slowly, slowly, a little bit more.

You break the juice
Gumming away
Til bits get loose
In your mouth they stay

Eight

1 week...
1 month...
Then 3, 6... 8!
The growing, the developing
How is it that you have learnt so much already?
I have learnt too. The smells, the different cries, the foods
you do and do not like.
But I look back to when we first brought you home. Small
(though large compared to most), innocent, untarnished by
the world, unhurt by the prejudices of the world you have
been brought into.
So pure.
So perfect.
And you have learnt to be a part of this world.
And I have learnt to protect you from it.
But together we go out and learn some more.
And as you continue to grow and develop some more, I can
only hope that I continue to do the same.

www.ingramcontent.com/pod-product-compliance
Lightning Source LLC
LaVergne TN
LVHW050506210726
843509LV00015BA/3010